Money, Money, Money!

Written by Laura Dargie and John Parsons

Contents		Page
Chapter 1.	*Unusual Allowance!*	4
Chapter 2.	*Bartering Goods*	8
Chapter 3.	*The First Money*	14
Photo Feature:	Coins	16
Chapter 4.	*The Last 500 Years*	21
Index And Bookweb Links		32
Glossary		Inside Back Cover

Chapter Snapshots

1. Unusual Allowance! Page 4

Imagine getting seashells, salt, or stones instead of your allowance! Thousands of years ago, these things *were* used instead of money!

2. Bartering Goods Page 8

People also used to swap things among themselves, instead of using money—but a better system was needed!

"An even

3. The First Money Page 14

In different parts of the world, a great advance was made: coins were invented, and people realized that this method of buying and selling things was much better!

4. The Last 500 Years Page 21

Banks, checks, credit cards, and automatic teller machines have changed the way people use money. And in the future, our bills and coins may seem as old-fashioned as seashells, salt, and stones do today.

better system was needed."

1. Unusual Allowance!

How would you like to be paid a handful of large seashells instead of your allowance? How would you feel if you received a bar of salt? What would you do if a large, twelve-foot wide stone wheel was rolled into your room on allowance day?

What Is Money?

Money is something of value that can be used to buy goods or pay people for their work.

Paying In Salt

About 2,000 years ago, salt was very valuable because it was used for cooking and preserving food. Roman soldiers were often paid in bars of salt, which they could then either use or swap for other things. We refer to this custom when we use the word "salary" to describe the money that someone earns. It comes from the Roman word for "salt!"

Coin Collecting

While we all like to have money to spend, some people collect coins and bills as a hobby or a job. These people are called "numismatists." Some rare coins and bills are worth tens of thousands of dollars!

If you had lived a thousand years ago, you would have thought that a stone wheel was just fine for your allowance. In those days, if someone had given you a handful of coins or a five-dollar bill, you would have wondered what they were!

Because coins are made of metal, they last a long time. It is possible to collect coins from thousands of years ago!

Long ago, seashells, bars of salt, and large rocks were all used as money. These things could be used to buy goods, such as food or clothing, and to pay people for work done. These items had a value that people in different parts of the world had agreed upon. They were a type of money.

How Long Does Money Last?

A $5 bill lasts about seven months before it gets too scruffy to use. A $100 bill lasts about three years, because it doesn't get used as often.

In 1988, Australian scientists developed a polymer, or plastic, banknote that lasts much longer. It is also better than paper because it is harder to copy, or "forge." This banknote has clear areas and small reflecting parts, like a hologram, that make it almost impossible to forge. Polymer bills are now used in Australia and New Zealand.

An Australian $50 polymer bill.

Today, the materials we use to make coins and bills are not worth as much as the value of each coin or bill. Coins are made of inexpensive metals and cost only a few cents to make. The paper or polymer bills used for larger amounts of money are also very inexpensive to manufacture.

Different Currencies

The type of money that is used in a country is called "currency." Each country has a different name and symbol for its currency.

Australia, New Zealand,
United States: . . . . dollar   ($)
United Kingdom: . . . . pound   (£)
France: . . . . franc   (F)
Japan: . . . . yen   (¥)

What Are Currencies Worth?

Currencies from different countries are worth different amounts. The difference between the value of currencies is called the exchange rate, and it changes every day.

As of August 1999.

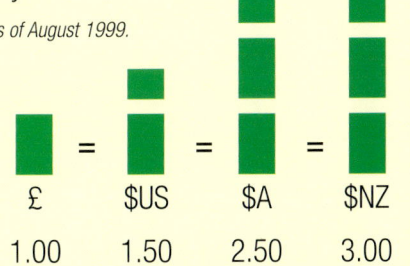

£	$US	$A	$NZ
1.00	1.50	2.50	3.00

One UK pound (£1) would buy two dollars and fifty cents ($2.50) in Australia.

The government of each country has agreed on a value for each coin and bill. Their value is easier to recognize and use than the value of other objects, such as seashells, stone wheels, or even gold and silver.

2. Bartering Goods

Before money was invented, people used to swap objects they thought had a similar value. If a wheat farmer wanted some chickens, he needed to find a chicken farmer who wanted some wheat. Then both farmers had to agree how much wheat to swap for each chicken. It was sometimes difficult to agree on what goods were worth so that both farmers could be satisfied with the deal.

This system of swapping things was called bartering. On the walls of Ancient Egyptian buildings constructed 4,500 years ago are pictures and writing that describe bartering. From these descriptions, we know that bartering was used in Ancient Egypt at that time.

If the goods that you needed were not produced in your area, you had to travel long distances to swap with other people the things you had grown or made.

People who lived around the Mediterranean Sea, which lies between Europe and North Africa, traveled hundreds of miles by land and sea to barter goods.

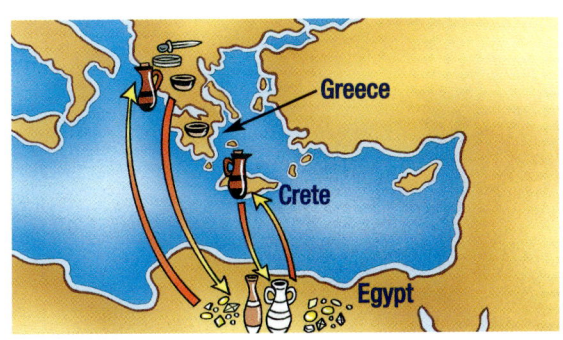

People from Greece and Crete transported olive oil, pottery, and metalwork to Ancient Egypt and swapped them for valuable vases and precious jewels.

The Romans, who lived in Italy, swapped olive oil, wool, and wine for spices from Arabia, gold from West Africa, wheat from North Africa, and silk from China.

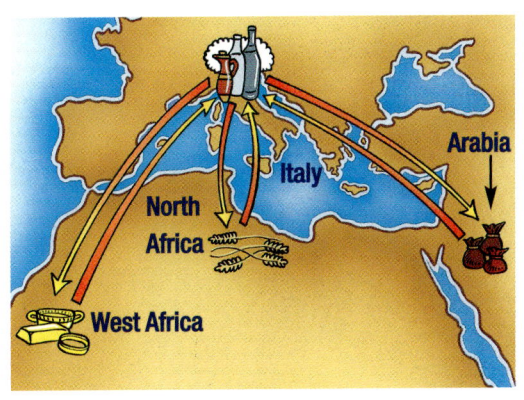

If the people you were bartering with didn't want your goods, you couldn't buy anything from them. People realized that a better system was needed—a system that used objects that could always be swapped and that always had the same value.

Everyone agreed that metals, such as gold and silver, could be used. So about 4,000 years ago some people started paying each other in gold and silver.

Bartering was used in many places for a long time, but slowly it became more common to use precious metals to buy and sell goods. However, bartering is still used in many places around the world today.

Gold

Most gold is mined from rocks deep underground. In many parts of the United States, Australia, and New Zealand, gold has been found as tiny grains in river beds. Three-quarters of the gold produced today is mined from rocks in South Africa. About 200 tons of rock have to be mined to produce only one pound of gold. But it's worth it—one pound of gold is worth more than $100,000!

Grains of gold and silver were carefully weighed out and used to buy and sell goods.

Silver

Silver is another metal mined from deep underground. Silver is a soft metal, so it is usually mixed with other metals to make it harder. Sometimes large amounts of electricity can be used to make silver cover other metal objects. When something, such as a dish or a vase, has been covered with silver, we say it has been "silver-plated."

Another common use of silver is in photography. When silver is combined with other chemicals, it changes color when it is exposed to light. The film we use in cameras is covered in a light-sensitive silver mixture.

Ancient-Egyptian paintings on the walls of buildings constructed 3,500 years ago show gold being carefully weighed out on scales. The paintings tell us that by this time, gold was being used as a type of money in Egypt. The more gold a person had, the more goods he or she could buy.

Every time a person bought or sold something with gold, he or she had to carefully weigh out the metal to make sure you paid the right amount. Every shop owner had a set of scales to make sure they were paid enough gold. It was easy to make mistakes, and some people cheated by adding weights to one side of their scales. An even better system for buying and selling goods was needed.

Ancient Price Lists!

In southern Iraq, ancient stone blocks covered in writing have been unearthed dating back to 3,500 years ago. When the writing was translated into a language we could understand, we discovered that the stone blocks were actually ancient price lists. They revealed how much barley, sesame oil, or wool a person could buy for a certain weight of silver.

An Ancient Egyptian wall-painting showing gold rings being weighed on scales.

3. The First Money

The First Coins

Three thousand years ago, the people living around the Mediterranean Sea began to use coins made of such precious metals as gold and silver. Coins were always the same weight, so people knew exactly how much gold or silver they were being paid.

An ancient coin from Iraq.

In Turkey, the first coins were small pellets marked with a simple design that indicated the coin's weight. But it didn't take people long to figure out that they could shave tiny pieces of metal off a pellet and no one would notice. If people sliced several pieces off several pellets, they saved a lot of money!

An ancient coin from Greece.

An ancient coin from Rome.

An ancient coin from Iran.

How To Stop The Cheaters

To prevent people from cheating on the weight of coins, governments began stamping their coins with the symbol or a picture of their rulers. It would show that they guaranteed the weight of the coin. Today, governments in each country guarantee the value of the coins and bills.

Governments also prevented people from slicing off the edges by cutting tiny grooves around the edge of each coin. We still use that method today on some coins, even though the metals in our coins are not as valuable as gold or silver.

Clever Coins

In China more than 4,000 years ago, an even better system had already been invented. The Chinese had realized that it wasn't necessary to make coins out of gold and silver.

As long as everyone agreed that each coin had a particular value, they could be manufactured from *any* metal, even an inexpensive one.

The Chinese government made their coins out of iron and stamped them with a certain value. It was an ideal way to prevent people from slicing pieces of precious metal from valuable coins.

Chinese iron coins from the 1300s.

The marks on coins are made using a special stamp.

How Are Coins Made?

Blanks are cut.

↓

Edges are rimmed.

↓

The blank coin is burnished to add shine.

↓

The blank coin is stamped.

↓

The newly minted coin is bagged.

Brand new coins, ready to be bagged and used.

Mints

A mint is a place where new coins are made and issued. Every mint around the world is carefully controlled by the government of that country, so it doesn't make too much money. In the United States, the Bureau of Mint makes and issues new coins. In Australia, new coins are issued by the Royal Australian Mint.

Special Edition Coins

Often, special edition coins are made in a mint to celebrate an event or a person's achievements. These coins can become very valuable to coin collectors because very few are made. They are not usually used as money.

These three special coins are:
1. The Susan B. Anthony silver dollar;
2. A Presidential gold coin;
3. A sales award coin.

Unusual Coin Shapes

Birmingham, England.

New Guinea.

The Philippines.

Ceylon (now Sri Lanka).

Thailand.

Mexico.

Heads Or Tails?

Tossing a coin is a popular way of deciding who will start a game such as football, basketball, or baseball. The "head" of a coin is the side that has a picture of an important person on it. The opposite of "heads" is "tails," of course!

Paper Money

A thousand years ago, the Chinese invented another money system. Carrying so many coins around was a problem, especially if you wanted to buy something really expensive. People needed many horses to carry sacks of coins! So paper money was invented.

An old paper note from Tibet (now part of China).

Strong Pockets!

Without paper money, you would need very strong pockets! If you wanted to use 25 cent coins to pay for something that cost $100, you would have to carry 400 coins to the store! However, if you used a $100 bill, you would only need to carry 1 piece of paper!

Unfortunately, paper money was not only easier to carry around, but it was also easier to copy! People who copied paper money were known as forgers.

The governments of countries that used paper money had to use many different paper-printing techniques to make the paper money difficult to copy.

Nine hundred years ago, the Chinese government started to use special paper and began to print its paper money in color, to make it harder to forge. Each note was printed with its own number, called a serial number. This made it easier to find out whether a note had been copied.

Designs on paper money are purposely complicated to make forgery very difficult.

The same serial number appears twice on each bill.

A Bank of England £20 note showing its metal strip.

Watermarks

Some governments now use "watermarks," which are special designs pressed into the paper, in addition to serial numbers. Some paper money also contains thin metal strips. These features are very hard to forge!

Euro!

In 1999, several European countries, including France, Germany, Belgium, and the Netherlands agreed to all use a single currency called a "Euro." Using euros will make buying and selling things much easier in the different countries of Europe.

4. The Last 500 Years

Banks

About 500 years ago, the first banks opened. Banks are places where people can safely store their money or borrow money if they need to. The bank lends the amount needed and charges some extra money for its use. That extra money is called "interest." In many places, banks started to print their own paper money.

Flowchart: How People And Banks Make Money!

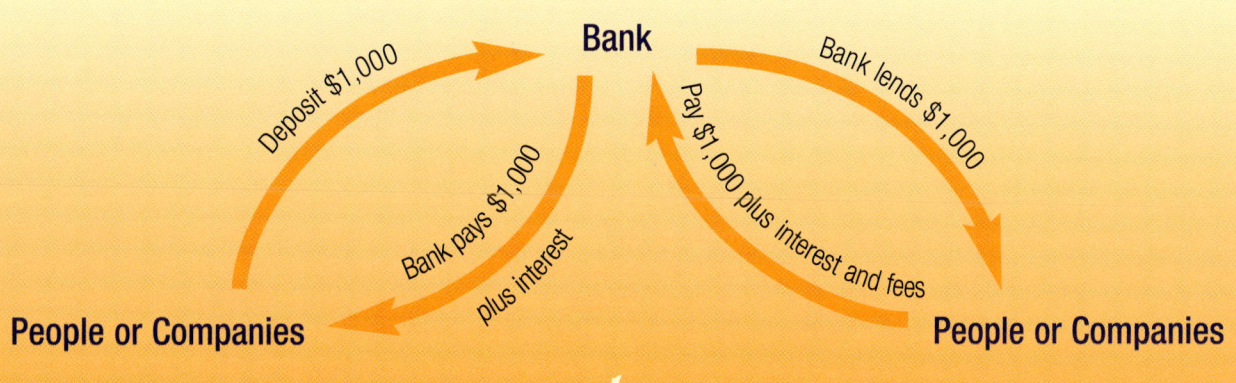

Checks

As more people deposited their money in banks, they realized that they didn't have to use coins or paper money all the time.

Checks are a common way for people to buy things without using coins or paper money. A check is really a legal note telling a bank to give a specific amount of money to the person or company who has received the check.

On checks, you write the name of the person or company receiving the check, the amount of money you want the bank to pay, and the date. Finally, you have to sign the check to authorize, or allow, the bank to pay that amount of money.

The Check Trail

Person 1 gives Person 2 a check.

Person 2 deposits the check at the bank.

Bank sends the check to a clearing house.

The clearing house examines the check and verifies the account balance of Person 1.

Bank's computer transfers money from the account of Person 1 to the account of Person 2.

Clearing Houses

Clearing houses are large organizations in which checks are sorted and processed.

At the clearing house, every check is examined to ensure there is enough money in the person's bank account. The signature on the check must also match the signature in the bank's records.

If there is enough money and all the information on the check is correct, the bank's computers transfer the money from one account to the other.

Because there are so many checks written out every day, it can take up to a week for the clearing house to authorize, or "clear," each check.

Credit Cards

About 50 years ago, an easier way to buy and sell things without using coins, paper money, or checks was introduced. The first credit cards, invented in America, were small plastic cards with a name and a special identification number pressed into them.

Today, credit cards are popular. Each time someone uses their credit card to buy something, the shopkeeper sends the details of the purchase to the credit card company. The credit card company then pays the shopkeeper the amount that the cardholder has spent.

There's A Limit!

The bank usually sets a limit on the amount of money a person can spend on each credit card. That means the person can't just keep on spending and spending!

Each month, the credit card company adds up how much money the cardholder has spent in places such as stores and restaurants. Once the cardholder receives his or her monthly statement, they have to make only one payment to the credit card company. Many people don't like to carry a lot of money around, so credit cards are popular.

Later, a small magnetic strip was added to credit cards. The magnetic strip contains information about the cardholder and the amount of money he or she is allowed to spend. It also enables the shopkeeper to dial into the credit card company's computer to process the payment immediately. All you have to do is sign your name on a credit card receipt to show that you agree to pay the amount charged.

Safer Credit Cards

To protect cardholders, banks ask people to sign the back of their credit cards. Signatures are unique to each person and are difficult to copy. Some credit cards also carry a small photograph of the cardholder on the back.

When Can I Get A Credit Card?

You have to be eighteen years old before you can apply for a credit card. If your parents already have a credit card, you can apply for one when you are sixteen—but your parents have to pay for everything you buy!

Automated Teller Machines (ATMs)

Banks also issue plastic automated teller machine cards that people can use in special computers to withdraw their money. ATMs were first used around 30 years ago and today they are in almost every city and town around the world.

The magnetic strip on every ATM card contains information such as your secret password, or PIN number. Having a PIN number means that only *you* can withdraw money from your bank account. That's why it is important for cardholders to memorize their PIN numbers and to not tell anyone else!

ATM Security

To protect people using ATMs, banks often hide cameras in the machines. If someone tries to steal money from an ATM, they will be photographed. If a person tries to use someone else's ATM card with the wrong PIN number, the ATM will keep the card.

What does PIN stand for? Personal Identification Number!

ATM Cash

ATMs can contain thousands of dollars—but when they run out of bills, they automatically shut down until a bank worker fills them up again. On weekends, the ATM sends a telephone message to the bank worker at home. That person then has to go to work and refill the machine.

Some vending machines also use this same system!

Debit Cards

Pretty soon, it will become even easier for people to spend money! Twenty years ago, New Zealand banks developed a system in which computers could swap money between different accounts at the press of a button. That technology will be available soon in North American cities.

Store managers now install a special wireless computer in their shop. When a customer uses their debit card in it, computers will transfer the money instantly from the customer's account into the shopkeeper's account. These special machines are called EFTPOS.

People can also buy goods and services on the telephone, using credit cards. Some bills can even be paid by using the numbers on the telephone as a kind of computer keyboard.

What Does EFTPOS Stand For?

Electronic Funds Transfer at Point of Sale! In simple language, that means the money is transferred by computers from your bank account to the shopkeeper's bank account, and it all happens immediately at the place where you are buying something.

With more advanced technology and better computers being developed all the time, using coins and paper money has become less important.

Still, it is nice to receive your allowance in the form of coins and paper money. And 4,000 years of inventing better ways to buy and sell with money means that we know how much money is worth.

And we should always be grateful that clever people thought of a better money system than seashells, bars of salt, or large stone wheels!

And In The Future?

Already, engineers are developing supermarket carts that automatically add up the money you have spent as you place items in them. And scientists are working on "smart" refrigerators and microwaves that will reorder foods directly from the supermarket when you run out. All you have to do is type your bank account number onto a panel on the cart, refrigerator, or microwave, and it will automatically send the money to the supermarket!

A Money Timeline

- **4,500 years ago**
  Ancient Egyptian hieroglyphics show bartering taking place.

- **4,000 years ago**
  People start to pay for goods with gold and silver. In China, iron coins are invented.

- **3,500 years ago**
  Scales are used to carefully weigh gold as a form of money.

- **3,000 years ago**
  People start to use coins in the Mediterranean region.

- **1,000 years ago**
  In China, paper and paper money are invented.

- **900 years ago**
  Paper money is printed on special papers using colors to make it more difficult for forgers to copy.

- **500 years ago**
  The first banks are opened.

- **50 years ago**
  People start to use checks and credit cards as well as money.

- **30 years ago**
  ATM cards are used to transfer money between bank accounts and to buy goods without money.

- **20 years ago**
  EFTPOS machines are installed in many New Zealand shops, and by the late 1990s are being developed in North America.

- **The Future**
  A cashless society?

Index

Africa 9
allowance 4, 30
Arabia 9
ATMs 26, 27
banks 21, 22, 23
bartering 8, 9, 10, 11
checks 22, 23
China 9, 15, 18, 19
clearing houses 23
coins 5, 6, 14, 15, 16, 17, 18, 22
credit cards 24, 25
Crete 9
currencies 7
dollar 7
EFTPOS 28
Egypt, Ancient 8, 9, 12
Euro 20
forging 6, 19, 20
franc 7
gold 7, 11, 12, 14, 15
government 7, 15, 16, 19
Greece 9
interest 21
Mediterranean Sea 9
mints 15, 16
notes 5, 6, 18, 21, 22
PIN number 26
polymer 6
Romans 4, 9
salary 4
salt 4, 6
scales 12, 13
seashells 4, 6, 7
serial number 19
silver 7, 11, 12, 14, 15
South Africa 11
Turkey 14
yen 7

Bookweb Links

More Bookweb books
involving money!

Juliette, The Modern Art Monkey—Fiction
The Grumpy Millionaire—Fiction
Big Gold Mountain—Fiction
Inspector Grub And The Fizzer-X Spy—Fiction
The Great Egg Problem—Fiction

Key To Bookweb
Fact Boxes
☐ Arts
☐ Health
☐ Science
☐ Social Studies
☐ Technology

32